Plainsongs

Editor

Eric R. Tucker

Associate Editors

Becky Faber, Michael Catherwood,
Eleanor Reeds, Ali Beheler

Cover art by Chris Goedert

Hastings College Press | Hastings, Nebraska

Subscriptions to *Plainsongs* are $20.00 annually for two issues, published in January and July.

Plainsongs welcomes submissions. The manuscript deadline for the Spring/Summer 2020 issue is December 15, 2019. Contributors will receive one free copy of the issue in which their poem appears.

Please use our online submission manager, available on our website, to submit work. Though we will endeavor to consider both e-mailed and snail-mailed submissions, these are not our preferred submission methods and we cannot guarantee responses for such submissions. All other correspondence can be e-mailed to the editor at plainsongs@hastings.edu or addressed to the editor at

> *Plainsongs*
> Hastings College Press
> 710 N. Turner Ave.
> Hastings, NE 68901

Plainsongs is indexed by Humanities International Complete, EBSCO Information Services, 10 Estes Street, Ipswich, MA 01938.

ISBN-13 978-1-942885-72-6

ISSN 1534-3820

Notes from the Editor

Thank you, gentle reader, for taking the time to pick up and peruse the latest issue of *Plainsongs*. There are many other things you could have picked up instead of this journal: a phone, an interesting-looking rock, a spatula, two spatulas, a full-color advertisement for the new 2020 spatulas, and a few other things besides. But here you are, at this very moment, casting your focused gaze *Plainsongs*-ward. We feel fortunate to have you with us, especially given the myriad responsibilities, entertainments, and distractions that vie for your attention every day. Do you ever feel as if the relentless barrage of electronic stimuli—the targeted ads, the e-mails, the breaking news, the Facebook updates, the inane tweets, the ceaseless blather and bluster, all those bright, flickering screens—has frayed your consciousness to the point of…not being…or not knowing how to…to be unable to, uh…

See that rock? The one next to the perfectly good 2018 spatula someone threw out? That rock has *sparkles* in it.

As does this issue. Here, you will find scintillating award poems by Rich H. Kenney, Jr., Thomas DeFreitas, and Matthew J. Spireng; insightful essays by associate editors Becky Faber, Michael Catherwood, and Eleanor Reeds; luminous cover art by Chris Goedert; and a cavalcade of poems so resplendent with imagery, ideas, emotion, and lyricism that you will be unable to avert your gaze.

Amid the din, we can lose sight of how much beauty there is in words. Poetry helps us remember; it reminds us of the power and aesthetic pleasures of the living language. In her poem "Remember," Joy Harjo, the new U.S. poet laureate and the first Native American to hold that post, writes, "Remember all is in motion, is growing, is you. / Remember language comes from this. / Remember the dance language is, that life is. / Remember." Go on: turn the page. Let's dance.

Eric R. Tucker, editor

Contents

Mimeograph Blues 8
    Rich H. Kenney, Jr.

About "Mimeograph Blues"
(A *Plainsongs* Award Poem) 10
    Becky Faber

Detox 11
    Thomas DeFreitas

About "Detox"
(A *Plainsongs* Award Poem) 12
    Michael Catherwood

Flagman with Cane 14
    Matthew J. Spireng

About "Flagman with Cane"
(A *Plainsongs* Award Poem) 15
    Eleanor Reeds

Secondhand 17
    Yvonne Zipter

Dubuque, Iowa, "Masterpiece on the Mississippi" 18
    Seth Thill

Reading Ellen Bass 20
    Aaron Leininger

Her Beauty Was Equal 22
    Karen Morris

When She Told Me 23
    Cecil Morris

A Dream of Wyoming 24
    John Garmon

How to Turn the Other Cheek 26
    Emilio DeGrazia

Epilogue 27
    Josh Mahler

I Stare at My Hand Until I Go into a Hypnotic Trance 28
    Milton P. Ehrlich

Necessary Lies 30
    Bill Glose

A Montana Message 32
    Travis Truax

Rekindle 33
    Beth Oast Williams

Emptied Nest 34
    John Sibley Williams

Rape as Character Development, or when I became a plot point: 35
    J. Rossi

remember me like this: 36
    Chelsea Balzer

And Yet 38
    Richard Luftig

Potatoes 40
    Lucy Adkins

The Tureen 41
    Doug Van Hooser

Bellevue 42
    Melissa Knox

The Smoker 43
    Elsa Bell

#dismantlingthepatriarchy is the new black we wear on wednesdays 44
    Kym Cunningham

Basket Weaver 46
    Mary Ann Meade

From the Mattress on the Floor under the Flaming Sky Photos 47
    Lyn Lifshin

The Ghost 48
    John Brooks

Foot and Mouth 50
    Josh Dugat

Specimens 51
    Hollie Dugas

Cinnamon Pie 52
    Katrina Hays

Dole Whip 54
    Kayla Murray

Waiting for Rain to Stop 55
    Jayne Marek

Sunlight 56
    Jim Dwyer

Untitled 58
    Sudie Nostrand

Museum 59
    Kathleen Mitchell-Askar

Understanding Superstition 60
    Lane Chasek

To Change I Need to Dig 61
   George Such

Green Ghazal 62
   Mike James

The Quarry 63
   Phillip Howerton

What's What: Keeping Things Straight 64
   Joan Hofmann

The Ventriloquist 66
   Judith Skillman

Albert 67
   James B. Nicola

80s Love Song 68
   Kevin LeMaster

Hope 70
   P M F Johnson

Sparrows in Early Spring 71
   J. Weintraub

Japanese Vase 72
   D. Marie Fitzgerald

Dead Tracks 73
   Alifah Omar

Xeruloid Mushrooms 74
   John L. Stanizzi

Freshman Year 75
   Mark Lilley

Pocket Charge 76
   Gabriel Ostler

Red-shouldered Hawk 77
   Nick Conrad

Midlife at Midnight 78
   Sue McElligott

place of death: field 80
   Sheree La Puma

The Ruts of Highway 58 81
   Carol Krauss

Soldier 82
   Diana Devlin

The Crow 83
   Psyche Torok

Nothingness 84
   BD Feil

A Metaphor for You 85
    Todd Johnson

Farm Life, A Litany 86
    Marilyn Dorf

Uncle Summers 87
    Heide Brandes

The House of Childhood 88
    Ute Carson

Moving On 89
    Liza Neal

Night Terrors 90
    Sharon Whitehill

Cat Person 92
    James Croal Jackson

Cigar Rings 93
    Lynn P. Elwell

Man on Church Street 94
    Emily Jahn

Mission Suicidal 96
    Scott Blackwell

CPR 98
    Maureen Sherbondy

* 99
    Simon Perchik

Float 100
    Ruth Holzer

Appearances 101
    Joseph Murphy

Silk 102
    Alice Pettway

Morningtime 103
    Suzannah Kolbeck

How It's Made Ep 9, Season 80:
"Birthday Cake" 104
    Michele K. Johnson Huffman

Waiting to Be Seen 105
    Martin Willitts Jr.

Mimeograph Blues

English grammar tests
came in blue—rolled
right out of a machine
Miss Goodloe called
the mimeograph,
grade school
standard-issue
back then.

I can still see her fanning
freshly run paragraphs,
the sheets reeking
in chemical bouquet.
Those in the front seats
sniffed out apostrophes
and compound predicates,
leaving back-seaters
with pronouns
unscented.

It was the year
I double-desked
with Alvin Underhill,
who told me he couldn't read
because what he saw in his alphabet
looked like letters in fender-benders;
that reading was like riding
a bumper car that ricocheted
off consonants and rear-ended
objects of prepositions.

When graded papers came back,
no one saw the skid marks,

the rubber left on mimeo—
not even Miss Goodloe's
red cross markings
that bled through
his test onto mine,
her note reminding him,
*A dependent clause
cannot stand alone ...*

but did back then.

Rich H. Kenney, Jr.
Chadron, Nebraska

About "Mimeograph Blues"
(A *Plainsongs* Award Poem)

Despite many moves during my adult life, one book I have never jettisoned is my copy of *Warriner's English Grammar and Composition*. It contains every bit of grammatical knowledge that one could ever need. "Mimeograph Blues" centers around the intersection between the rules of language and the way in which they don't work for every person.

The structure is developed nicely. Stanza 1 lays out the concept of the use of a mimeograph for reproducing the tests, thus setting a visual sense as well as the upcoming pressure of examination.

Stanza 2 brings in a first-person focus as a witness to "her fanning / freshly run paragraphs, / the sheets reeking / in chemical bouquet." While those in front "sniffed out apostrophes / and compound predicates," as readers we see that what happens at the front of the row doesn't necessarily make it to the back of the row where the pronouns lack the chemical odor.

The third stanza brings the tighter focus that brings in two powerful concepts—Alvin's illiteracy and his beautiful metaphor of the bumper car vision of letters. The similes in this stanza are perfectly developed.

The connection between the speaker and Alvin, initially noted by the fact that they were "double-desked," becomes more intimate once we know that "Miss Goodloe's / red cross markings / …bled through / his test onto mine…."

The bleeding of the red ink leaves us with a stronger sensory concept than the mimeograph odor. Miss Goodloe's note about a dependent clause is, again, perfectly chosen to encapsulate Alvin's plight. At this point, it is obvious that the "Blues" of the title goes beyond color in meaning.

Becky Faber
Lincoln, Nebraska

Detox

A hurt woman of thirty, thirty-five,
doing a seven-day stint at Pine Grove detox
paces, hazy, puzzled to be alive:
feet wedged in flip-flops, sheathed in dirty socks.

Her voice is Castle Island, her first name
a common one for children of the '80s.
She clings to the few comforts of this Hades:
cigarettes, decaf coffee, shared shame.

Red-haired, her face all freckle and tear-streak,
familiar as Broadway or Andrew Station,
she manages both defiance and defeat.

I ponder the sad mystery of her feet
scuffing the Lysol'd halls of desolation
where she'll get sober if only for a week.

Thomas DeFreitas
Arlington, Massachusetts

About "Detox"
(A *Plainsongs* Award Poem)

In Thomas DeFreitas's "Detox," readers are taken through a maze of details that capture the painful fight of a young woman confronting addiction. DeFreitas uses the sonnet form to navigate the tight avenues of agony, grief, and hardship, all with a finesse the subject demands.

"Detox" explores the complexity of addiction and recovery: "a seven-day stint at Pine Grove detox" is probably too short to change a behavior. The prospect of defeat lingers throughout the poem. The speaker's tone approaches doubt and at the same time sympathy in the poem. After the first quatrain, the descriptions move into personal details of the woman: "Her voice Castle Island, her first name / a common one for children of the '80s." The clinical tone of the speaker creates a distance that gives the voice authority. We don't learn the patient's name, and with the prospect of a failed treatment, there's an implied toll the speaker has endured in witnessing defeat as the patient "clings to the few comforts of this Hades / cigarettes, decaf coffee, shared shame."

Especially admirable in the poem is the ability of the writer to use a sonnet, often a poetic form of love and admiration, to detail the hardship of a detox patient. The texture of the form increases the emphasis on the subject and paints a vivid and unromantic tableau of human struggle. The form never overwhelms the subject as the poet's skill is deft in creating many lines that are enjambed and images that are fresh and surprising. After the volta (turn) in the second quatrain, the speaker tightens the focus on the patient: "her face all freckle and tear-streak." And a line later: "she manages both defiance and defeat."

In the final tercet, the first person "I" suddenly appears: "I ponder the sad mystery of her feet / scuffing the Lysol'd halls of desolation." There is uncertainty that hovers over the treatment; the speaker has seen many failures and is somewhat weary. But there is the fight. Success cannot begin without taking a step forward, an action away from addiction.

Michael Catherwood
Omaha, Nebraska

Flagman with Cane

I dared not stop to ask
and tie up traffic, so
I can only surmise, but

I'd hate to think it was
the fault of a driver
who disobeyed or was

confused and hit him
so now he's even less
agile, less able to leap

from the path of a car
coming right at him.
Seems foolish to me,

and he seems clumsy,
cane in one hand, red flag
in the other, a hobbling

matador hoping for
that last bit of glory
as he waves his flag

for cars to stop or
pass, hoping always
to avoid the horns.

Matthew J. Spireng
Kingston, New York

About "Flagman with Cane"
(A *Plainsongs* Award Poem)

I decided upon this poem because the image created in its last two stanzas imprinted itself on my brain and would not be dislodged. Across a stanza break, the flagman becomes "a hobbling // matador," a stubborn survivor facing down the "horns" once again. A "clumsy" figure whose situation "seems foolish" becomes ennobled when the speaker begins to see him as a doomed hero, persisting futilely in the face of terrible odds.

The image of the matador succeeds in becoming more real than the person that inspires it as the poet's unexpected association captures a moment precisely by sidestepping it. "Flagman with Cane" recalls Ezra Pound's perfect distillation of imagism in "In a Station of the Metro": "The apparition of these faces in the crowd; / Petals on a wet, black bough." In his poem, Matthew J. Spireng offers the second half of such an equation even more sparsely—with only two words that specifically register this new image—as the penultimate stanza opens with "matador" while the final stanza closes with "horns."

The poem builds carefully to this epiphany of vision, ensuring that it is both a revelatory surprise and an earned payoff. The title announces what has prompted the speaker's train of thought, a speaker whose hesitancy and uncertainty—"I dared not… I can only surmise… I'd hate to think"—gives way to an imagined scenario that prompts guilty laughter. The simplicity of the language makes the poem feel conversational and even conspiratorial as the speaker confides in us about this bizarre scene. The line and stanza breaks suggest pauses in the retelling of this anecdote as we are left waiting for the suggestion that follows "but" and sustaining the instinctual "leap" out of oncoming traffic that the flagman cannot perform.

"Flagman with Cane" reminds me not only of modernist poetics but also of Dickensian character portraits. In *Our Mutual Friend*, for instance, a solemn policeman walks and talks more like a friar while one can only truly grasp the stern sway of a pub's landlady by envisaging her as a school teacher. Spireng's eye is as paradoxically indulgent and critical, drawing on all the resources of imagination to discover the sublime matador lurking beneath the skin of the ridiculous flagman.

Eleanor Reeds
Hastings, Nebraska

Secondhand

The Sixth on Lawrence Avenue offers
a cocktail infused with smoke:
cedar, citrus, molasses-soaked tobacco.
But I prefer the old way: the honeyed voice
of Chet Baker drifting lazily like the blue smoke
of a red-tipped cigarette in an ashtray,
making the light and my senses hazy and mellow,
the sweet sadness curling around me
with every note until I am a little dizzy
and the ice in my glass is as misty as I am.

Yvonne Zipter
Chicago, Illinois

Dubuque, Iowa, "Masterpiece on the Mississippi"

City of celtic cross tattoos,
of twenty plus Catholic churches
and thirty plus bars and pubs,
of 45 dollars in bail money
for my brother's public intox.

City of muddy river water and fishfly stench,
of towering bluffs and peer pressured hikes
where my feet stole the skyline's view

City where Abe and I street performed on Main.
City where Abe and I were cited for performing unpermitted
 on Main.

City of old men wearing workboots
in gas station checkout lines disgusted
by a woman paying credit for a one dollar fountain drink,
not realizing she had 30 dollars in diesel
before he frothed at the opportunity to be angry.

City of early winters and late springs.
City whose levees defended us from the Mississippi
through the Summer floods of 2008.

City my father never escaped,
and city where he and my mother gave me life.
City where we prepared to move in with Grandma
in case his paychecks couldn't pay the mortgage.
City where they always could.

Dubuque, I write to you with no plans of return,
but in hopes of no more motel meth lab explosions.
In hopes you shield my loved ones from lessons

I learned in puke stains on your concrete.
In hopes that the brush covered limestone in my brain,
the irish blood in my veins,
and the Christian guilt in my chest
will always buy my memory a place
amongst the lightning bugs
and fishflies.

Seth Thill
Cedar Falls, Iowa

Reading Ellen Bass

Ellen's right, of course,
we should probably be reading Neruda—
although, the world may or may not revolve
around domestic tables.
Either way,
that *life is heavier than the weight of all things*
I know well enough already—
but is reality only our measure of sorrow and loss,
numbed by the comforts of repetition?
I wonder,
does she know what it's like to work for a living? the
    succession of days
become as flat and as gray as the pavement—
that burn your soul away, like a utility?
and if praise is insufficient testimony
to such a fate
then surely there is occasion for song,
and semi-
dangerous folly—

as all that aspires, or evolves, moves wildly upwards—
while the command of living lies
in continual change.

Are we the body only,
blood and bone—a godless idol
bound only to this round of days? Perhaps,
it is not our obligation, then,
to advocate our loss—
as gravity begs for no assistance.

And maybe domesticity is not for everyone, Ellen,
as some find no redemption

here in its shallows,
or in the dishwater of ordinary days.

In spite of sidewalks and city planning, vile weeds bloom
in wild variety
giving themselves away to the sun—
while even the dead may be still
dreaming in their graves,
aspiring toward surface things and light
like a blind stem
opening on a field of new images.

Aaron Leininger
Redding, California

Her Beauty Was Equal

When her beauty was equal in magnificence, not to rage
but to secret weaves and intricate plaits that transformed the nest
of her hair into a basket of gorgon knots atop her impenetrable head,

she was a magnet for scents, of pheromones for pheromone seekers
in a butterfly dress. And who is not a pheromone seeker is not alive
but dead. Just look at her ordinary face, emotions neutral—

for no one but herself. Poised above unremarkable eyes, a set
of question marks fine as filament or twin antenna to signal balance—
without want for camouflage, before knowledge of the spoiled seeds

and how they're scattered—carried on bare feet and painted toes
in loving marriage to the earth; before sugar-cane and servitude
and ravages of every bloody-thing-else that happens up the road.

Karen Morris
Narrowsburg, New York

When She Told Me

The clunk after clunk of the knife brought down
through hard carrots, deliberate, forceful—
the chop through orange root to cutting board, chop,
the vegetable split to finger food size,
ready for dipping, nibbling, slow ingestion:
that's how her words felt going in my ears—
thunk then thunk then slices of me split off,
and I could not speak, could barely breathe,
and she continued cutting, each stroke firm
and sure and right down to the wooden base.
And then, when she was done and I silent
still, she started humming and left the room
and I sat down and tried to breathe again
and gather all the slivers back to me.

Cecil Morris
Roseville, California

A Dream of Wyoming

Children of the Middle Ages,
People of rain gullies
Follow water spots on windshields
Into thermal seasons under Yellowstone,
A triangle of light
Accumulating, slowing down, turning
Until shadows break hard.
The curling sky along the diagonal
Makes a sharp right and pulls over
Into new states called Idaho and Montana.

As sad as Pompeii and fleshed
Against the ready fruit of fall,
Dipping into curves at twilight
Above ancient cliffs, the shore
Disguises a continental shelf,
Below the beach we walk the waterline
Up the shallow dunes
Towards shoals where breakers rose.

Peaks of the Bear Tooth Range
Turn blue with sun and ice
As wind blows dust around us.
We are like creatures in a tide pool.
On the surface the sky, the clouds,
The reddish cliffs are shining.
The first real scorcher of summer
Brims on the tentacles of misting rain.

A shroud of gauze envelops our path
As if we are standing alone on a treeless
Prairie, ready to face the autumn wind,
Shortly before midnight, when archeology

Tries to harness the boulders in the dark
As they do their subjective work far below
The flat fields where coasts once surged
Against the dying, gorging land.

John Garmon
Las Vegas, Nevada

How to Turn the Other Cheek

1.
Stiffen your jaw
Against the latest barrage of sun-baked belief.
Let its words shatter against hard bone.
Take deep breaths to let blowback gather strength.
Hide your spit beneath your tongue.

2.
Lay yourself in the lap of desire.
Let your mind lose itself in its fragrant folds
Until you close your eyes and sleep comes.

3.
Surrender jowl and jugular
Unconditionally to the fanged beast.
Relax when he sinks his teeth in you.
Imagine yourself as virginal.
In the spiked thrill finally achieved
Gaze wide-eyed at the calm pond,
The delirium of warmth draining down.

4.
Be a leaf
That rights itself
As winds blow away.

Emilio DeGrazia
Winona, Minnesota

Epilogue

When opening the door to an empty room
and feeling yourself alone, walk in without

turning on the light. Let the moon shine in
thru the blinds onto the bed, let it spread

over the carpet—the blending of the night
with whatever the morning will offer. Go in

and lean against the wall, your ear barely
touching the cool paint, lobe like a compass

with the weight of the soul pointing down.
Lean in and follow the near distance where

the tangible body joins with your shadow.
There are places between life and death—

the trickery of our eyes as proof of darkness,
the familiar eyelash of light before we sleep.

Josh Mahler
Centreville, Virginia

I Stare at My Hand Until I Go into a Hypnotic Trance

Hypermnesia triggers vivid memories.
Grandma gives me a shiny new penny
which I stick into the gumball machine
at Earl's candy store, and I retrieve
a winning blue and yellow gumball.

Earl was also my scoutmaster.
His face was full of twitches and tics,
with a hemangioma on his cheek
the shape of the Catskill Creek.
The owner of our only candy store,
he lived with his scoliotic old mother
in a few grungy rooms in the back.

We met every week in a dingy church basement
with a bleeding crucifix on the wall.
Pilgrims from Krakow claim he wept tears of blood.
Earl drilled us like an army sergeant,
barking: "Line up. Left face, right face,
about face, and forward march!"

A master of tying all kinds of knots,
he taught us how to tie a clove-hitch,
sheepshank, sheet bend and bow-line.
He supplied us with bunches of lollipops
and licorice pipes at camping jamborees.

After each meeting, embraced in brotherhood,
he became teary eyed as he led us in Taps:
"Day is done, gone the sun, from the lake from the hills,
from the sky, all is well, safely rest, God is nigh."

No one could explain why he hung himself
on a lamppost in an alley behind the store
with a perfectly tied hangman's noose.

Milton P. Ehrlich
Leonia, New Jersey

Necessary Lies

This won't hurt a bit, the doctor says,
foot-long needle filling his fist,
faith in anesthesia absolute
from his side of the table.

Dawn lies face-down
in an open-backed smock,
slats of her ribs stark
as a white picket fence.

Beneath her armpit,
he thrusts with all his weight
like a brute
breaking down a door.

And as her hand
vises mine, I wonder
how much of life's passage
is greased by lies.

When my fifth grade class
cut apart frogs, pinned
skin to trays, plucked out
hearts and other organs,

our teacher promised
that the dead
would not reanimate
and haunt our dreams.

It takes this moment
beside my girlfriend
laid out on butcher paper
like a landed fish

for me to understand
these lies are spoken
to soften
our own pillows.

And so I pat her
trembling hand,
whisper in her ear
how much I'm sure

the biopsy will be negative,
how life will soon
go on as it always had,
how outside the window

a gray-cheeked thrush
is whistling just for her

Bill Glose
Yorktown, Virginia

A Montana Message

after William Stafford

Moving here, we pulled
the mountains around us,
close, kept the south
best we could, hidden alive
in our coats and diction.
We kept what mattered,
living here with love,
no longer letting the hands
of greed peel away
our gold, never allowing
the mountain mine to uproot
the way the creek bends
and sings. No longer
chasing stars, looking up,
no longer hiding. We tell
everyone, we are here.
Come, friends. We can
show you how this place
has evaded most trouble.
Most, I say, only most,
for there are errors, of course,
everywhere, the reservations,
the dams, poisoned wolves,
the greed we can't erase.
What's beautiful isn't perfect.
And isn't that a home?
The undercurrent we've
connected with,
by habit, by heart,
holding our lives against
the stone? Come, now,
we will have to show you.

Travis Truax
Bozeman, Montana

Rekindle

Against a backdrop
of exposed brick, the new
owner shoots a selfie,
smiles flash-quick,
as the mortar loses
its grip on a crumbling wall.

Windows crack with a slanted
smile, a taunt of *I dare you*
lingering. Dust fogs the cellar
like leftover cigar smoke,
matchbooks still littering
the mahogany bar.

In the air floats a faint scent
of something close
to burning, a pot left
too long on the stove,
the house struggling to spit
fire in the face of change.

Life here lasted until brisket
fell off the bone, the ember
of a Cole Porter song scratched
itself down to nothing,
the man in the room no longer
making Mama so hot.

Beth Oast Williams
Norfolk, Virginia

Emptied Nest

Times when paper cranes unhook from the sky
& drift back down to us, flightless, or those nights

the pillow we share seems an entire universe
in miniature: sweat-rimmed memories that may

not be true, lost hair, lost languages, the aftertaste
of desire. Everything painted the wrong palette.

Like pavement after the rain evaporates. Like light
from a neighbor's window, the life backlit within.

On the map of our bodies, a star-bright city
a wrist-width away from the last. Pencil-thin

roads leading toward & away. Commonplace oaths
that lose themselves in translation. No ceremony

in it all. In watching the night's mouth widen into dawn.
In counting the bird-shaped shadows on the walls,

suspended there, silent, having clipped the strings.
In the flight implied. That beautiful stringless flight.

John Sibley Williams
Milwaukie, Oregon

Rape as Character Development, or when I became a plot point:

You know, I only do it to grow you,
the character—it's not personal
it's just very effective, actually maybe
historical, yeah—historical

Have you learned enough? Have you
grown? Because if not, I can do it again

and again and again—I can make your
face every woman's face and just
you know, grow you—until you are a
better, stronger version of yourself,
just a little more complicated.

I hate to say you were asking for it,
you needed to be broken before you
could be strong, so just let me break you

and remember, I'm doing this for you.
For the story, for the reader. For me.
Keep watching, this scene really makes it.

I don't do this for fun, you know.

J. Rossi
Burlington, Vermont

remember me like this:

squatting
to piss,
all
paper-bag colored
from our
grabs at early
summer,
wearing your
old work shirt
next to the
misconstrued creek
I used to pick
mulberries behind
when I
thought that just
stomping on things
made them
wine,
beside the
govern
ment-
sponsored fields
of endless
corn & soy,
still self-made
& mysterious
to me,
staring at the
birds we only now
notice, black with
bright
orange
shoulder pads,
warning each
other of the in-

coming storm that we
risk letting
soak us,
downhill from the
bench you discovered
years before
sharing,
the one that you
like because it's
easy to miss,
which holds
still at the center of
loose gravel roads,
bike paths,
concrete high-
ways like tangents all
huddling near the
small bits of
wild that
survive through the
not-really-looking
of cars going by
as I'm
crouching,
bare-assed &
surviving this
way too,
close to the
earth so that
just you

can
see
me.

Chelsea Balzer
Omaha, Nebraska

And Yet

> *Because I know that time is always time*
> *And place is always and only place.*
> —T.S. Elliot, "Ash Wednesday"

Yesterday I saw two lone daffodils
out by the toolshed, their heads
poking out of the earth like newborn
twins. This morning, I must report
they looked a little discouraged.
But that should not be surprising
to anyone who has spent time here:
Indiana in early April
has its way of breaking your heart.
It is what happens in this land,
this life, often at odds, often askew.

Here where the winds blow so hard
that sometimes rain seems never
to touch the ground. How strange
that it is winter that tempts us,
convinces us to try to live again
but also, not to poke our heads
out too soon or become cocky,
like these fallow fields all full
of false bravado; dead, toothless
husks with their kernels gone missing.

And yet, and yet,

we have learned how we must
make do in this only time,
this always place, where perhaps,
if we are lucky, before the days
become too long again,

the wind that takes our breath
away will again spark and fan
new life when we least expect it,
and where things can take courage:
this sun, these fields of unborn corn
the newborn daffodils by the toolshed;

You. I.

Richard Luftig
Pomona, California

Potatoes

He was traveling from Chicago
to Joliet, he said, on the expressway,
Old State Highway 59, when a
semi rollover caused a load of potatoes
to scatter across the road.

People stopped, pulled their
pickups and jeeps, their Chevy vans
and VW bugs off to the shoulder,
got out and dashed across three lanes
of traffic after Idaho russets and
Yukon Golds, reds and whites and yams.

I'd have understood if it were
a Brinks truck with flyaway tens
and twenties. But potatoes?
Perhaps it was the fact of
sudden bounty dropping down
in front of you, and like unexpected
grace, you must be grateful,
whatever it is that is given.

Lucy Adkins
Lincoln, Nebraska

The Tureen

Or whatever it is, came from Sicily.
    The ceramic ugliness a swaddled baby
        so it wouldn't break like a heart. Why
else carry the memory across the ocean's
    pitch and yaw? It had to have a meaning
        similar to a wedding ring, but their children
Americanized. Their immigrant status
    faded photos except for the oldest, the language
        did not melt on his tongue. We move three miles
and I save the tureen from a dumpster dive
    even though the soup was eaten long ago. You
        and your siblings do not know why it made the
            trip,
but hunger gnaws in my empty stomach.

                              Doug Van Hooser
                              Naperville, Illinois

Bellevue

In the bed where you sit, voices dim, whispers
You turn to hear

Ulysses bound to the mast,
Straining toward the beauties who will drown him.

The hallways teem with harpies,
Malodorous, untied hospital johnnies flapping

Backsides unwiped,
They hiss across scratched linoleum
Wanting to hear.

You hold your head and ask
If I will bring you a hat
Since you want to become a policeman.

A nurse, round as the white pills she offers
Smiles, watches you sip and swallow.

Ulysses, wax in his ears,
Speechless on a pillow.

Melissa Knox
Essen, Germany

The Smoker

Outside in the mist, wrapped in a long overcoat,
hatless, the smoker
stands, gaunt as an ancient tree.
Each day from this patio, he gazes
over traffic and clouds, noting the changing
shapes, the movement of the sun.
There isn't much else to watch from here.

His fist uncurls to strike a match,
long fingers lifting it
to the cigarette's thin tip.
Like birds, his delicate hands
flutter to shake the match flame out.

Something precious seeps from that thin white stick,
filling cells like liquids,
smoke uncurling rich and innocent
as steam from tea.
The smoker's hands rise to his lips again and again,
steady as a fine watch piece,
out in the frost, out in the rain and snow,
every day this spot,
every day at three.

Elsa Bell
Indianapolis, Indiana

#dismantlingthepatriarchy is the new black we wear on wednesdays

with the cleverest of signs and proud pink hats
we match la croix with the flavor profile
of today's outfit to forget
we sold our virginity
for a crochet bikini and a blood diamond smile
#adultingishard we swear
on gluten-free sacrament
that smells like day-old organic milk
sipping carbonated half-truths from company soda
we wake denim-clad to wait in line
for the road less-traveled while playing pickup sext
covered in ironic sweat
we'd like to burn our bras
but lost them and our marbles
at a deserted festival last month
plus we'd paid $95 to feed
the little brown hand-
stitched brands someone said
celebrities weren't wearing yet
we'd never admit
we check our phones to know our place
weighing words in finsta likes
fishing in smaller ponds where water shifts like cruel
    intentions and
we swab our cheeks to prove the dreamcatchers
on our backs aren't appropriation
but lost culture recycled in google image searches
shouldering complicity in vegan restaurant's leather bombers
and memories of impoverished youth while
irritated, we question others' foodstamp stories
we never dumpster-dived for shelter
but we can still smell aldi

on hand-me-downs
and bring a quarter to rent public school shopping carts
learning relativity in suburban poverty
where morality charges flesh by the pound
and bodies are a buyer's market
we try to sell, but find independence is worth less and the
    only i
in happiness we've stabbed a wooden stake through
heavier than the splinter we try to remove
from yours
we wish we believed
in anything enough to feel
free to consume ourselves

Kym Cunningham
Austin, Texas

Basket Weaver

Over one my breathing, far down into the weave.
For am I not the wind to the dry shoot of willow.
Am I not the wren, making nest after winter nest.
Though I sense someone coming on the back road.

I hurry on, *under one over one*, my hand pressed
Into the weave. For the weight of light has broken
The worn handle of every wicker basket. Falling
Over a bent shoot. I answer the knock at the door.

Who comes to take the wind, if not the wren.
Who but the town reaper who in haste has cut
to the root the last row of willow. *Over one*
or is it *under.* Town reaper, I have lost count.

Mary Ann Meade
Lansdowne, Pennsylvania

From the Mattress on the Floor under the Flaming Sky Photos

rain blurs moon
and dark, eyes dark
as licorice or water
in an old mine. A
stranger reading
Lorca in Spanish on
the phone. Later my
hands smelled like
him, cinnamon
skin. The dog barked
thru damp sheets.
I got wet, fingers
on my skin. *"you all
horned up."*
If I'd thought
twice I wouldn't
have in my leather
skirt and high
heels, pink *"what
are those,
barrettes?"* he
asked pulling rose
clips from my hair.
"And your scent," he was
pressing the strangest
flowers, pulled
my hair, tilted
forsythia dripping like
my hair, as I fell out
of what held me

Lyn Lifshin
Vienna, Virginia

The Ghost

I arise to August
mist. You're gone

again; some plane
somewhere. I make

a myth of you, bury
you in a wooded lot

on your knobby side
of the river, pull the rib

from a stem of strong
grass, pretend it is

your spine and snap
it in two. Bluegrass

voodoo. Not sure
if you're really dead

or even if that is
what I want. It'll go

the way it goes. Darling,
this reflects my zeitgeist.

You left me in Rome, wet
in fountains. Don't correct

my geography. I, too, embrace
the unknown alleyways

of the world, commit to
the absolute danger of living.

This is dude ruin. Conjure
the ghost and the ghost

appears, all your life
I bet.

John Brooks
Louisville, Kentucky

Foot and Mouth

We watch him split the hoof in half,
a brittle head of garlic held
for me to whiff: a sour tear
that takes the rotten fossil's shape.

Hobble falters. That is not
the crippled trot of cattle
streaked from heel to hock in pink.
They lurch and fall. They molder.

Options stir and fester.
There were shots and ointments.
Now he lifts a matchbook
from his pocket and he

plucks a cardboard sliver.
Sulfur sweetly blisters,
and like recognition
I remember healing

follows hurt and so
I go on singing.

Josh Dugat
Tuscaloosa, Alabama

Specimens

I preserve omens
because they are bound
to the *goodness* and *badness*
of earth—little-legged
models of heaven and hell
that turn up to guide me
tingling in my clutch
as I pose each limb
and eye-spotted wing.
It's reverence if I say it is
as I drive a single nail
through the abdomen
of each prophecy,
pinning the carcass
to a small wooden cross
where it hangs restless
awaiting examination.

Hollie Dugas
Las Cruces, New Mexico

Cinnamon Pie

Your hand reaches into the jar and scoops
one tablespoon to tell the story of how
your husband, The Colonel (my great-great
grandfather, Lieutenant Governor of Nebraska,

Civil War veteran, pioneer), always had to have
two different kinds of pie
for his mid-day dinner. I like to imagine you
as irritated, not desperate, on some raw March

morning one hundred fifty years ago when
you looked into the larder and saw nothing
to make another pie, no new dried fruit appearing
overnight, no nuts, no meats, nothing

for the damn second pie. I like to think
a little grin danced across your face when
your eyes lit on the spice jars; that you thought
to burn his mouth a little, jolt his head

up from his plate to see you. Maybe
you hummed to yourself as you concocted
the simplest of fillings: sugar, water,
flour, salt, and cinnamon; perhaps you had a little

giggle on that dreary sub-zero Midwest
morning, cows bawling in the darkness outside.
"I'll give you two pies," I want you
to think as you carefully poured the liquid

into the bottom crust (the same flakey
crust I make today, the recipe handed down
my father's line to my mother, to my sisters, and me.)
And later in the day I see you serve him

that pie with a vindictive twinkle, see you watch
him bite into the hot red spice— But your hand
was too generous with the sugar,
Great-Great Grandmother Belle,

because I know when that man first tasted
the pie I am making today, his stern face
lit up for an instant, and even though I bet
he only gave you the briefest nod,

I think you tucked it away, to be taken out
later and examined, as I examine
the faded, spidery handwriting
on the back of your photo.

Katrina Hays
Bend, Oregon

Dole Whip

you spread fresh-ground almond butter
on semolina & seed toast
you spread the laundry across that bulky
primitive-print chair and fold neatly

you spread your hands across mine and they
feel like a paper weight on my paperwhites
you spread out brie and shiny crackers for us
on a porcelain blue plate from Japan

you spread out, dole out words in ink because
you think you mean something written down:
'I miss you
my mind is swimming with thoughts of you'

you spread other girls' legs
and on a tainted mandala bedspread where I broke hymen, conceived our baby, amniotic fluid broke,
milk let down, I let down and broke down with fluidity`

you spread a smile only to the small corners of
your lips, because it's filled with contempt

I've put all these moments down on mental spreadsheets, but cannot fill the blank frames
so I'm going to be a self-fulfilling goddess and spread
paper hearts across the floor to trample them

spread African black soap across my body
and your charcoal toothpaste on my teeth
and maybe drink one of those lavender
charcoal lattes to cleanse

I'll be spread across supple,
but I will not be spread thin.

Kayla Murray
Jacksonville, Florida

Waiting for Rain to Stop

Its insistence comes as a surprise,
gray sky without an armhole.

The unwrapping sounds outside the window are gentle
but not from pity. Against your impatience
it teases, as if you,

a child, quaked to become adult.
That coat may not fit your shoulders,

every decision a scrap and a stitch
of tailoring that frames you in the world,
that may not deflect the rain.

Yews gnarled with their knowledge
and humble crocuses with eyes shut

during the long dimness—
their clothing is the chill
acceptance that sews them into place.

Jayne Marek
Port Townsend, Washington

Sunlight

a break in the clouds
a burst of sudden surprising brilliance
the Great Miami dazzling & wild
the radiance of shattered sunlight
all those tiny flashing kaleidoscopes of color
like the scattered remnants of a broken
stained glass window from the cathedral
of Our Lady of Ecstatic but Tragic Love Affairs—
beauty is made of time (time is made of time)
only what's dead is eternal & still
the clouds like my thoughts are restless
they just cannot stay put
that brief moment of blue is going going
gone & now (watch it you can't control it)
the sky returning to deep February dismal
the river circling back to its more
usual lackluster late winter condition—
cold flat dirty brown slash
drab olive drab—
the colors of fuck you very much
if you can't take a joke
the colors of maybe
we'll make it to spring
but maybe not but either way
the traffic on Main never stops
the rules the wheels within wheels
they are relentless
either way the shit keeps on
rolling down hill
either way your life & mine
the chaos of chance plus
the choices we have to make
either way what's sacred is not

invisible jive & razzmatazz
not the holy word of some God revealed
the sacred instead is flesh bone blood human
the struggle for justice & freedom
the work of practicing compassion
no matter the daily falling short
the wearying litany of loss & defeat—
hope is an act of love
love of course is crazy
love is one of the choices
you can make when the drugs quit working
love is the only way
we can possibly learn it
how to be good for nothing
love is what creatures
like us get to do
because we are not divine…

                                    Jim Dwyer
                        St. Petersburg, Florida

Wealthy women
climb stairs in Vienna

to the offices
of Sigmund Freud.

They wait
in velvet chairs

for a consultation
in the small room

with one window
and his African artifacts

lining the book shelves.
Here they pay him

to be taught
to mistrust their inner selves.

Sudie Nostrand
New York, New York

Museum

Human forms behind glass suggest living
she kneels in snow there
forms a face of a face she says is hers

whatever she has kept
from me
made that cold body
bare   pared down
forehead and eye socket
rise out of her erosion
depression's glacial scrape
furrows and lines the cold skull
taking shape beneath her hands
tell me
about the underside

My fingerprints all over the pane
between us
bloom and contraction of fogged breath
Her native heat
buried so deep now

Kathleen Mitchell-Askar
Elk Grove, California

Understanding Superstition

You can't want happiness.
Between depression and just becoming
happier than usual, dilemma blossoms
like a violent cluster of hibiscus flowers.

The salt I toss over my shoulder
isn't for luck, it just distracts disaster.
If you need to ask why a superstition
survives, you need to quit questioning

and let the bones roll, even if one
is your skull on a silver platter.
The luck I have isn't the same as my luck
yesterday. The more I try to better

my luck, there's no luck awaiting
what I call the hereafter. If you want
the true meaning of broken ladders,

shattered mirrors, modern art,
or black cats missing tails and feet,
step back three feet, proceed forward
two more and no more. There.
You're right where I want you.

Lane Chasek
Lincoln, Nebraska

To Change I Need to Dig

The word *arroyo*, with its double-r
trill, rolls off the tongue like the rush

of water through a gulch, and how much
I'm like the *tierra,* unable to escape the way

torrentes gush through the channels carved
in me. How my *arroyos* give me away,

showing all who notice, the *carreteras* cut
by rain, the *carreteras* that fill when it pours,

the *carreteras* that overflow in storms, water
naturally moving to the lowest place.

George Such
Baytown, Texas

Green Ghazal

Every fence, yes, even white picket ones, are built for staked claims
And fears. Keep your neighbor's apples out. Keep your world within.

It's easy to be sad in front of a fence, even if your default setting is joy
Mixed with bliss. I want to climb any fence. Sit beside crows. Settle in.

Who said grass always looks greener on the other side? Please provide
Answers through first class mail. Feel free to include cash for good will.

At any fence you can stand at a gate and guess who gets in. You can also
Hand out clown-faced balloons. Maybe offer reheated wisdom, with a grin.

Out west, some fences seem to have no end. Walk all day, only cows for
Company. Shout at the sky when lonesome. If there's an answer, it's wind.

Mike James
Murfreesboro, Tennessee

The Quarry

The rolling hills and Brown Swiss
never made the grandfather
or the father rich, but the son
was determined to make the farm pay
at any cost. He saw thin dirt
as an obstacle to his fortune
and sold topsoil to blast limestone.
He soon made fools of the old folks
by turning rock into gold. The newspaper
visited but couldn't mine enough superlatives
out of the English language to express
the benefits and beauty the Chamber
of Commerce saw in his operation.
He related for readers again the story
of how the family had toiled
and of how only he had succeeded.
But the people he speaks for are gone,
as is their place of struggle and life,
and gravel trucks circle like buzzards
as they spread the farm upon
the new four lane north of town.

Phillip Howerton
West Plains, Missouri

What's What: Keeping Things Straight

Gray rounds
ironed to smooth
sit in tableau.

Count them,
eyes tracking:
It's not easy.

Nestled bunches
glossed over
by running tide

Brackish water
salt, not salt,
evening their skin.

Each holds itself
and others,
like family.

She'd said she'd *had
6 children & about
13 grandchildren.*

13 and 6 sound
right. It's *about*
that's out of place.

A dozen would sound
too casual, glib. 13
would sound accurate.

About 13 grandchildren
Sounds off-handed,
Like *could be, maybe.*

Even glacial rounds
Deserve to be counted:
One, two three…

Joan Hofmann
Collinsville, Connecticut

The Ventriloquist

Later, when the voice in his belly
is not loud enough to make him
sick, he explains to the grass and trees
how she wouldn't go away.

Sleep was a problem for her.
She wore a kerchief
and spoke Greek,
her apron always spattered

with ink from irises.
Whenever purples grow too heavy
and topple over
he feels less like a prophet.

Her mop of curls, her broomstick legs,
it's not that he misses her simple body
made of wood. Nor does he think
analysis could cure

her complaints, nor stop the adrenalin
that flowed between them continuously
as attention. A summer
more ragged than pretty,

and he's popping up like a cork
from the dusty water
of her drowning
to the surface of his sheets.

Judith Skillman
Newcastle, Washington

Albert

My friend is the epitome of grace
and yet writes poetry about abuse.
You wouldn't know by looking at his face

that some soul must have dropped from outer space
and lit upon his person to produce,
by magic, an epitome of grace.

I can't tell if he's ever had a base
thought, or the least desire of tearing loose;
you couldn't tell, by looking at his face,

the hell he's lived through, either: there's no trace
of rage! But in a way he's a recluse
for, after all, epitomes of grace

are enigmatic, difficult to chase,
no less befriend, relax with, or seduce.
Yet every time I look upon his face

it's all that I can do not to embrace
him, or to tell you, when I introduce
him, that he's the epitome of grace,
though you might know it, looking at his face.

James B. Nicola
New York, New York

80s Love Song

Stray Cat Strut does
    its familiar
shuffle through every ear pressed
    against a car radio,

and at that precise moment

we realize we know nothing about
    love; its mystery, lain bare in
the backseat of my 60s Chevy.

we dance the horizontal bop
    in secret shadowed hallway
and back alley, on bended

knee, we cry

for the insatiable more,
    and swear it is our song,
except when it is hers, until its

resonance

means nothing to either of us,
    and when our hungry eyes lock
at midnight and her curfew is

over,

I lend passion
    to the next willing soul, ready to drink
the half-dark paradise by the dashboard

light

For the night is young and so
are we, and only the young can say.

Kevin LeMaster
South Shore, Kentucky

Hope

That which we may and
that which we do too often stay
strangers, like a condensed film
of coming dangers where no one
speaks our common tongue and
every hero labors in a different country.
It's tricky. Bring down too much stone
from the pillars in that first take,
we are ourselves crushed, not just
the zealous one. (Listen carefully,
you hear the desperate mice
in the walls, the roll of dice.
Not everyone bets with the director.)
When failure happens, we say the projector
malfunctioned, or play the rushes
proving none of us was stricken down,
and anyway, all recorded properly.
Too often, we lack reel pluck.
We whistle away gut emptiness
as mere bad luck, score in some
poor-me songs—Lola Beltran, say—
and tell ourselves well, at least
we made a competent serial rerun.
Yet, some insist if we atone for
damage done, aid others in stitching
together their own impossible bodies
from the shamble of parts, stick with
an honest script … and don't run,
this could be the movie where
lightning irradiates our resurrection,
when, after the beat of a snare
and some interceding divine fanfare,
the new heart starts.

P M F Johnson
Minneapolis, Minnesota

Sparrows in Early Spring

Feel free to ignore me and the crumbs I've spread around,
my friends of last fall, who would, whenever I sat down
to my breakfast on the quad, flock and then press and plead
with chirping and cheeps your sparrow's tale, and peck the ground
with fury for all those scraps I'd toss your way,
from the stalest bagel's crust to the smallest seed;
but fodder and feed are far from your minds
these glorious spring days when you can find
whatever you need without my help, and play,
instead, the game of love: fluttering wings
aloft, the flailing tail, the flight, the chase
that fuels the blood to flaunt feathers and sing,
display, to capture, build, and propagate;
my crumbs can wait, but just you wait until
the flowers bloom and you've got maws to fill;
just wait until the edges of those leaves turn brown,
and winds turn round from south to north to chill
the air to ice, and hunger gnaws; you'll look around
again for that brooding shade and beg for his spray of crumbs—
but for now, a drop of blood against a cobalt sky,
a male cardinal atop a sycamore lets fly
his sonorous peal for all to hear and for one to come.

J. Weintraub
Chicago, Illinois

Japanese Vase

For sixty years it moved with us,
that Satsuma vase.
Other objects disappeared over the years,
but the vase was always there,
the original design brought by Korean potters
to Japan in the early 1600s
to the island of Kyushu.

It fell once,
surviving a clean break.
Mom glued it back together.
She believed it worth something,
held this vase in awe:
the Japanese man and woman
in feudal dress,
bold colors of red, blue, orange,
the backdrop a seascape,
an island in the distance,
a three clawed dragon wraps
the circumference,
flamboyant figures in enamel
outlined in gold against chocolate
and white dotted moriage.

I can't remember when
we didn't own this vase
mother purchased at auction.
When she died it became mine.
It would have been the perfect
place for her ashes, but there
is no stopper or lid.

She is there though,
all the same.

D. Marie Fitzgerald
Palm Springs, California

Dead Tracks

Like cut-off tracks … no more
choo-chooing down
this path. ain't none
to be laid down again,
tryin' to cover the
entire countryside of my gold skin.

And he wasn't even sorry. said
he was afterwards as they always
do. because I didn't do what
I was accused of, I was
brandished and condemned:
a liar, a hoe.

Shit always seem
to be nearby to manifest, render,
some kind of punishment. was
it on the table? the counter?
cain't remember. jus'
hot off the fire …
those cookin' forks. you know?
the long ones for
babecuin' or pokin' meat.

Ahh!

It bit my left arm.
hot metal sinkin' through my flesh all
the way down
to my feet.
and my mind,
sizzle like hot grease
touched by water.
after awhile,
I ain't feel nothin'.

Alifah Omar
Merrillville, Indiana

Xeruloid Mushrooms

A small priory of monks visited my garden to chant very quietly in the moonlight. I didn't even know they were there. I noticed them in their tiny, unsheltered abbey when I walked to the garden at dawn, basil at respectful attention, the eggplant bowing reverently in their purple vestments.

John L. Stanizzi
Coventry, Connecticut

Freshman Year

After a few weeks together drinking *Old Styles,*
my new roommate begins to trust me—

first with the story of his father arrested
for shoplifting cigarettes, the shame

of reading about it in his hometown paper,
his mother trusting only in Jesus,

and then what he fears most:
his parents finding out he's gay.

He tells me he's known since he was twelve,
and that he needs more time before coming out.

But because he's been visiting those other bars
he's worried word might reach

his town, his neighborhood,
his father walking the dogs.

He wants me to imagine having just made love
to my girlfriend, the two of us

walking down a cobblestone road,
the night a storybook of stars,

and then having to let go of her hand
whenever we pass beneath a streetlight,

and I keep nodding the way someone does
who wants to understand but can't.

Mark Lilley
Fishers, Indiana

Pocket Charge

smaller arenas
make the biggest pops.
it's easier to get everyone
on the same page if the book
can be bound with a paperclip.
When you say, "I was born in the
wrong generation," discerning folk with a jeweler's loupe
    pointed at
your phonograph needle only hear, "The enormity
of the audience completely dwarfs my message."
Tough ticket. Grand stage. Back when there was more
to go around, you could get a primo gig by setting up
camp in a famous person's office and subsisting on staplers
until said individual got sick of trips to the supply room.
And you'd set off, touching down on parts of the crust
that felt new, enclaves of culture in this Anasazi hillside
we call "it." Now, what tells you that you're somewhere else?
I was there so quick and now I'm gone, into a duvet and
light switch easily found in the museum of leftover
humanity. Cells piled up on every surface, manufactured
in a time where people bought adult films on TVs and
intimacy meant something. Nostalgia
is nothing more than the world
being too big.

                                            Gabriel Ostler
                                       Orinda, California

Red-shouldered Hawk

The crescent moon,
skull white, yet steel blue,
hung like some double
bladed kramabit.

Under such a sky,
I wanted to think
that fall's austere
sentinel, beak shaped

like a scimitar,
was just waiting
for some clutched prey
to die. Not that it

had been so wind
buffeted during its
journey south that it
was forced to light

in a field shorn,
just yesterday,
of corn. I wanted
to say an eye

was kept on me
as my car slid by,
that some glance seemed to say
so much of living

involves such taking.
No, the hawk's gaze fell
beyond my ken. Then,
a sudden taking wing.

Nick Conrad
Sylvania, Ohio

Midlife at Midnight

I want to be beautiful
I want to be good
I want the wind to blow my hair around, and
my jeans to look like they did 30 years ago.

I want to be pretty
I want to be sweet
I want to play in the grass
while the sun colors my skin;
sprinklers, raining upon my t-shirt
like that of a young woman,
who need not care of
lines and bumps and shadows.

I want to be fun
I want to be funny
I want to hear the genuine laughter
that tickles the mind
and flutters the heart.

I want to be good
I want to be grown
I want the ageless moments
of everyday life to breathe
into my own breath,
without choking on age's
cruel tricks and deep regrets.

I want to be alive
I want to be grateful
I want to stand alone in
my own deep embrace;
looking in the mirror without pause,
without the silent judgment
staring back.

I want to feel
I want to not feel
I want another ride on
the road that led me here;
the pavement leveled bare
with new footprints, new secrets,
and a promise to
never need another wish
again.

                                              Sue McElligott
                                        Nevada City, California

place of death: field

Each minute, less sky
I know you watched the land
grow close.
Woke to find your toes
planted,
frothed with blood
as tufts of tall grass
rustled with wind.
Did you curse
the bright & unholy as
you left your heartbeat
there, your hands
punctured like tin.
Oh Grief.
Our daughters
search then find you,
hope scattered like seedpods.
They leave the wreckage
for the birds,
& weep.
There is a darkness
now, like a lunar
eclipse.
& every day,
less sky.

Sheree La Puma
Valencia, California

The Ruts of Highway 58

the trees were not blurred. each distinct. the knot holes, broken limbs, crumbling bark on the oak and the ruddy laced maple. i saw her weave among the trees, her skirt dragging mud spits, snagging on briars and evading berry tipped fingernails. she danced among the fog and mist of dismal swamp and i watched her from the backseat window. i wasn't surprised to see her. i wasn't surprised she was trailing after my car. she had been running recon on me for 58 years. whispers, shoulder taps, checks at the tracks before whistle warnings. that time on the trestle when I slipped on slick moss and boone's farm. netted me from plummeting into the french broad river currents and swirls. it was her boldness that surprised me. her threshold from my mind to running sentry. sentry among the wraith militia of the revolutionary and civil wars that surprised me. forest haints. i pressed my face to the cold pane and envisioned her jumping tombstones, broken sabers, and rattletrap cannons to ride me home as the nor-easterner bore down, pushed the car with fists of wind. swiped the car to the edge of the road where she simply held up her palms and with a flick of power guided the nissan back into the ruts of highway 58. wiped her hands on her white petticoat and glided behind a pine.

Carol Krauss
Portsmouth, Virginia

Soldier

In the pub he's a cathedral
of a man stretching tall
holding hard. A welder
tough as tungsten, Jack
leans on the bar
one hand in his pocket
keeps dead white fingers warm,
the other curls around his pint.
Laughs with the rest of them.
Jack's alright—like the others
in their prime.

The barman signals time—
slow shuffles, glasses tipped,
backs patted, Jack—tight lipped
feels his fingers tremble
glances at the clock
wills the hands to stop.
Remembers who he is,
how late it is, where he belongs.
The long walk home—
feet wade through tar, he knows
she's waiting.
This cathedral prays now
as the dark dissolves the man in him,
an egg without its shell
waiting to be beaten.

Diana Devlin
Dumbarton, Scotland

The Crow

It's hard to see in the pre-dawn light,
harder still with the overcast sky.
But I see now who you are.
You stand alone, like me,
an outlier of sorts.

You tolerate me
with my bag of food meant for
mallards: stale bread, broken
corn chips.
All I have are these scraps
but I chance an offering,
tribute to a disavowed warrior.
I approach cautiously, so as not to
alarm.

You look comical, almost fragile as you
sidle toward me. Your little stick legs
seem like they could break easily.

I know what breaks easily.
But you, black-caped and intrepid,
teach me endurance as you
scoop up the bread and take to
the air.

Clouds are flocking on the dawn like
spirits of avians ascended, and my eye
follows them as I call out,

Let me fly with you.

**Psyche Torok
Columbus, Ohio**

Nothingness

Already we've lost it if we must
Put a name to it. If we tilt the machine
To our favors, force dogged tabs into slots.
If we insist upon nomenclature.

It's no longer that crystalline thing.
But then, it never was that thing. That thing
Of primary color or right angle or straight
Line. Anything of matter. Any of thing.

Well. Even now I do not define it, do I?
It circles back into circle, and there
I go again. It is the thing impossible
To be named. Yes, it is the impossible.

BD Feil
Belleville, Michigan

A Metaphor for You

It's more important that I find
the diagrams to connect us
but I'm on the cold linoleum,
head beneath the sink, you
taking me through instructions
to the conundrum of plumbing.

It gets the better of me,
more than I could figure out.
Around my head is conduit
immoveable as myth; it rids
us of waste, lets us cleanse
our common objects once again.

Water—how much like love
I thought—and it was seeping
away. And what is more precious
than the ordinary compound
we need as it's mostly what
we are? We link its channels

properly or the simple stuff
we can't retrieve eludes us.
More is beyond our means
and I'm not grasping
the dynamics of the flow,
the mechanics that controlled

what was being lost. I rested
my head beneath these intricacies.
I was failing the task, a problem
I couldn't take a wrench to;
more to it than I could figure.
Clearly a metaphor for you.

Todd Johnson
Racine, Wisconsin

Farm Life, A Litany

Farm life is a litany
resounding in my soul,
    the mooing
    and the cooing,
    the cackling and the calling,
the early red-combed rooster
waking up the dawn.
    A litany, the competition of cornstalks,
each tough and slender shaft striving hard
to be the very first to touch its tassel
to the burning brow of sun.
    A litany, alfalfa fields
perfumed and purple-blossomed
as to crown the Prince of Wales.
    A litany, the milking,
true as mealtime, twice a day. And every day.
Cows humble and grateful, flashing
their tails come sun, come rain, come snow.
    A litany, the windmills,
taller than giraffes, purring and gurgling,
clearing their throats, each one in a different key,
as they obey every huff, every puff
of the roguish and rascally wind.
    A litany, the barns and sheds and silos,
honorable as servants grouped a stretch or so away
from the meek and humble farmhouse
where the master lives.

Marilyn Dorf
Lincoln, Nebraska

Uncle Summers

Watching you spit curses like "how's the weather?" and "pass the salt,"
I found you spread-eagled, jeans ripped like moth wings, sitting on the fence
dripping with the juice of apples and smelling like demons and cigarettes.
I knew what hunger was—a forked tongue kiss sweet with cider—
and I wanted to lick your wrists while you sang folk tunes to the chain link fence.

Lion man, you lying man, big with boasts and mouth stained in laughter,
you can take down an enemy with your sleeves rolled up.
But I am not your enemy and I am not your any "thing" anymore.
I have a hard time speaking to you, my tongue catching on consonants and
volleying the vowels around like heavy-finger fables and ghost stories.

Your fingers are black with motor grease, rotted cherries.
Carrying blue veins under paper-bag skin, the back of your hands
are hangman's nooses of mahogany bluster and beige backhands.
My jaw is dust under such waking breaking of bones.

Drunk uncle is a cliché, and you can only say pain
when your mouth is caught on the barbed wire.

Heide Brandes
Oklahoma City, Oklahoma

The House of Childhood

We return to the place
where we first heard voices,
smelled the air and tasted nourishment,
where hands caressed or frightened us,
where comfort was our cocoon
or neglect made us shiver.
The tears of harm are cold,
the tears of joy warm as a lagoon.
We carry the house of childhood within us,
and spying through its translucent walls
we keep life at a distance—or embrace it.

Ute Carson
Austin, Texas

Moving On

Loneliness comes at night
when the day of fuss and flurry
dips down
and the memories come
rubbing and drifting
like milkweed spiders
carousing through the dusty air
unseen, only felt,
a nudge
into once was
and isn't now.

left and leaving,
what once was
isn't ever gone.

Liza Neal
Northampton, Massachusetts

Night Terrors

Every woman knows
how it feels to go out
to her car late at night
on an unlighted street
feeling unnerved—
despite its locked doors—
by the possible man
who hides in the back seat.

Yet in my quiet town
neither my children nor I
lock the house, wouldn't know
where to look for the key.
Not unusual for us, one warm
breezy night as I walk
to the movies, to leave
windows and doors
open wide to the world.

What I do not foresee
is how sickened I'll be
at "The Fly"—how spooked
by the images, sticky as webs,
that cling to me all the way home.
They will haunt me for days.
Be afraid. Be very afraid.

Only streetlights illumine
dark rooms in my house,
create lacy patterns that flicker
prettily, gently, over the walls.
I suddenly think of the family
who not long ago were found
murdered just one quiet town
to the east.

My limbs liquify, my heart
is a hammer that bruises
my ribs. What red-eyed assassin
may be crouched in a corner?
What bloated insect hangs
from the ceiling, waiting
to drop?

I flip switches, flood rooms
with brightness, watch shadows
take flight as I lock every door—
terrified as a child so intent
on the safe zone of blankets
she dare not glance back.

I'm blood-curdled enough
to make my big husky Tess
precede me into the bedroom,
as panicked as when I left
my hospital bed in a drug-induced
dread. *Night terrors,* nurses assured.
Don't worry, nothing is there.

But tonight the terrors invade me
again. Though I later steal out
to unlock the front door
for my daughter, leave her a note—
Lock the door when you come in!—
she fails to see it and leaves
the door wide as a mouth
to suck in the sweet summer
morning.

Sharon Whitehill
Port Charlotte, Florida

Cat Person

You ask me to watch Marshmallow while you vacation
in Miami without paying me even though this is a definite
inconvenience but I oblige and then you text demanding

picture updates and a few hours after I say *I'll send one later
when I'm there* you ask for an update before I even arrive
like hanging out with your stupid cat is its own reward.

Look, I swear I'm a cat person.
I am.

But only with every cat I've ever lived with.
Before that, I was a dog person, gerbil,
fish. What I'm saying is I am adaptable

but your cat is not. Today I am swinging
by to swing scooped poop in a plastic bag
around the house and dump a confetti of

special urinary chickenmix into a small bowl
and there are flies all over the house from the
first night of catsitting because when I arrived

Marshmallow was nowhere including outside
and maybe I left the door open when I searched
everywhere shaking a bag of treats only to find

the cat was inside the bedframe, just hangin' under
the mattress in a clothesdrawer, only to immediately
sprint into a shoe closet and stay because Marshmallow

is not a person-cat, and oh my god look at you on the rug
cutiepie wants a belly rub yes you do ah god damn it
fucking fine.

James Croal Jackson
Pittsburgh, Pennsylvania

Cigar Rings

I used to wear my Uncle Charlie's cigar
bands on my fingers as paper rings.
They were red, white and green—
the colors of the Italian flag.

My Uncle Charlie was a homunculus;
a discarded beer-barrel torso perched
on two stubby legs—the spitting image
of H. L. Menken, including the cigars.

One Sunday afternoon, Uncle Charlie
was fixing my grandmother's fuse box
in the basement when he said that we
all would get a painful electric shock.

I crouched down next to the coal bin.
One time Uncle Charlie spun this yarn
that the FDA was poisoning our entire
food supply with secret toxins.

I didn't believe my Uncle Charlie then;
why did I believe him this time?

Lynn P. Elwell
Durham, North Carolina

Man on Church Street

Red rimmed eyes and white teeth
Flashing, a baseball cap
Pulled low, making shadows like

Corners of city streets.
His voice cracked hard and
Fast, filled with something

Impossible to describe, only by
Its negative space, what it left
Out; an inability to articulate

The gaps. Frustration and something
Else, maybe panic—
A profound sadness

On fire, the frothing edges of
The stillest sea.
Why can't we gift our worlds?

The inexpressible, those hidden
Watery depths, iridescent
And cold. Some hurricanes

Never reach the shore—
Rage and throw themselves
to pieces, raking their nails over

Indifference, all the creatures that might care
Protected, wrapped in waves
Under their glittering

Azure cage, colored like
The heavens.
And all the people on these

Lamplit streets like minnows
Darting through the wreckage—
The ruined decks of

Sunken ships, in and out of
Shadows, brushing the eaves
Of endless halls. If only lives were more

Like soap bubbles; I mean besides
Their fragility, but in ability
To share their gleaming

Borders, perhaps to drift a while
In tandem, mixing the air
We breathe.

I wish I could give.

Emily Jahn
Grayslake, Illinois

Mission Suicidal

The assignment is all mine—
improbable,
probably impossible,
immaculately opaque,
though I'm still trying to remember
whether I ever accepted it
or not.

I suppose this is the proof,
my death sentence signed,

sigh—
either way,
seems I was sent to record
this or that for
the home office, wherever it is,
and the orders are always vague,
too often
more scrambled than omelets,
transmissions intercepted
by microwaves
ultraviolet radiation
the Fox News network,

and I'm left out here, in left field
to welter in the sun,
make it up as I go,
twist in the breeze—
the funding nonexistent
along with the inspiration,
though I somehow keep
plodding
a
long—
the booze helps,

but then again
there is never enough of that …

I survive
by sheer animal instinct,
a stranger
on a strange world,
rerouted,
never meant for this destination,
but finding myself
nevertheless here,
fighting
for justice, democracy, world peace—
while okay, yeah, in a chair—
and while also avoiding the actual
human race
as much as possible,

but dutifully filing these reports
almost every day
for whoever would read them,
whenever and however
that might work out—
so much samizdat sent
by pirate radio,
too often on the wrong frequency,
invisible,
the channel forever changing,

in a code so arcane
even the Navaho still call it
nonsense,
comprising a transcript I doubt
will ever be understood
by anyone,
especially the author.

Scott Blackwell
Champaign, Illinois

CPR

I pass the room of plastic bodies,
piles of stiff, naked legs and arms
slanted at odd angles, painted-on eyes
staring at ceiling panels.

Some days students perform CPR
on their assigned mannequin models,
human lips press down on plastic lips.

Sometimes I imagine my students
are mannequins. Dull eyes
staring blankly at phone screens,
or heads dropped down on desks, asleep

as if no blood surged through
their veins. I want to open up
their lips, breathe life,
infuse fervor inside of them.

Maureen Sherbondy
Durham, North Carolina

*

There's still the smell from salt
—you bathe this pebble, sure its pulse
can be found close to shore and nourished

feel its way through a shallow sea
thriving on unhatched eggs from a stream
long ago extinct—you scrub side to side

as if all rock remembers hand to hand
a darkness starting to swarm in a sky
not yet breathing on its own, no stars

though what you hold up goes on to become
a death, bit by bit driven into the ground
covered over with running water and candles.

Simon Perchik
East Hampton, New York

Float

Along the pre-dawn streets
the milk float glides
in electric near-silence.
The gentle clink of bottles,
the whir of muted wheels
deliver to us as we surface
in the loosening grip
of nightmare or delight,
the recurrent promise
of a day like the others.

Ruth Holzer
Herndon, Virginia

Appearances

This poem is included in the author's collection
Shoreline of the Heart.

Our voices shimmer in the dreams
of a slumbering word; are a star-shaped map;
water under the keel
of petal's sigh.

Beneath the mountains' heart-shaped scree,
a sea swells through veins
of grass and weed.

What is as it appears?

Lies persist—pitch through an open door,
drunk and hoarse; maddened
by the world's spin.

They reach for my collar, my throat!

But I'm rising from my wounds:
unquenched; restless;
wanting to shoulder more; to be
as persistent as the emptiness
within a brick, a stone.

What is as it appears?

Sails are made of loam; moonlight
shines from the wheat's tongue.

Joseph Murphy
Colorado Springs, Colorado

Silk

I threw away
my stockings, even those

with no runs. Nylon
is no silk, but still—

the thought of worms
boiled to smooth my calves.

I've waded through
enough sacrifice already,

and which gown
in this closet is too fine

to ride my bare skin
on the dance floor.

**Alice Pettway
Shanghai, China**

Morningtime

God, it is beautiful here sometimes.
When the high, hard heat sweeps across the baked pasture
    grass
        To be tucked away at night with the setting sun;
When the first stars blink in the sky,
        Light in points jumping off the river;
When the sun returns at dawn,
        Shouting down the birds and waking up the lazy ants
            and bees;
When the rain pours a deluge,
        Turning the backyard into a bog
        And tattooing a steady rhythm on
        The shingles and peeling painted windows;
When the blankets stir beside me
And your hand fumbles through the crumpled sheets for
    mine,
Quiet as a leap of faith,
In the sleepy pre-day of morning time—

Before the dogs are fed and our girl is awake,
Before the insistent chatter of the alarm,
When I reach across the blankets
To meet your fingers.

                                        Suzannah Kolbeck
                                        Baltimore, Maryland

How It's Made Ep 9, Season 80: "Birthday Cake"

If we know of these
hidden processes of cut
glean press
these impressions slatted
onto/over raw material
then we know our whole selves.

Eating a cake that no human hand
has ever touched
until the baby flings
her palm into the pre-cut slice

Until my thumb grazes an edge
of frosting and I lick it away
taste the sweet gritty underside
of my thumbnail

The processes now *known*
unhidden, filmed, scripted
should bring comfort—what is asked of us
cut   culled
pressed into a tin gilded
in plastic

It's so easy! Find what you need
here! Find absolution complete
with spare time!
Find that your body
is nothing more than vats
and nozzles. Find that your hands
are mere objects

and your mouth
a hole.

Michele K. Johnson Huffman
Greensboro, North Carolina

Waiting to Be Seen

Light hazed in morning,
uncertain what color to choose
or if to blend them all,

without understanding that
if you mix all the colors
they become muddy.

Things vanish in fog,
making near-accidents.
That is why the geese are low,

shredding the fog. That's why
we hear their waning cries
long after they're gone.

The world is straining to be seen.

Martin Willitts Jr.
Syracuse, New York

Trust your instincts.

Subscribe to *Plainsongs*.

Name: _____

Address: _____
_____

E-mail: _____

- ☐ One-year print subscription ($20)
- ☐ Two-year print subscription ($35)
- ☐ Three-year print subscription ($50)
- ☐ One-year e-subscription ($10)

Please send check and order form to:
  Plainsongs
  Hastings College
  710 Turner Ave.
  Hastings, NE 68901

www.ingramcontent.com/pod-product-compliance
Lightning Source LLC
Chambersburg PA
CBHW022010120526
44592CB00034B/773